31143011512226
J B Love, K
Fishman, Jon M.
Kevin Love /

Main

Kevin Love

By Jon M. Fishman

AMAZING ATHLETES

Lerner Publications Company • Minneapolis

Lerner Publications Company
A division of Lerner Publishing Group, Inc.
241 First Avenue North
Minneapolis, MN 55401 U.S.A.

Website address: www.lernerbooks.com

Library of Congress Cataloging-in-Publication Data

Fishman, Jon M.
    Kevin Love / by Jon M. Fishman.
        pages   cm. — (Amazing athletes)
    Includes index.
    ISBN 978–1–4677–1881–3 (lib. bdg. : alk. paper)
    ISBN 978–1–4677–1892–9 (eBook)
    1. Love, Kevin, 1988—Juvenile literature. 2. Basketball players—United States—Biography—Juvenile literature. I. Title.
    GV884.L65F57 2014
    796.323092—dc23 [B]   2013000590

Manufactured in the United States of America
1 – BP – 7/15/13

TABLE OF CONTENTS

"Let It Fly"   4

Basketball Family   9

High School Hero   13

Big Man on Campus   18

Getting Better   23

Selected Career Highlights   29

Glossary   30

Further Reading & Websites   31

Index   32

Kevin Love *(center)* greets his teammates on November 21, 2012.

"LET IT FLY"

Basketball fans at the Target Center in Minneapolis stood and cheered with surprise on November 21, 2012. Minnesota Timberwolves **forward** Kevin Love had just come onto the court. This was Kevin's first game of the 2012–2013 National Basketball Association (NBA) season. He had broken a bone in his hand just two weeks before the season began in October. Most people didn't think he'd be back on the court until December. Not even Kevin's teammates knew for sure that Minnesota's star player would be back that night. "I didn't want to make a big deal about it," Kevin said.

Kevin warms up before the game against the Denver Nuggets.

Kevin is Minnesota's best scorer.

Kevin had called his father before the game. He told his dad that he was playing that night and asked for advice. "Let it fly," Stan Love said. Kevin took his father's advice to heart. He started the game on fire. He made **layups**. He hit **three-point shots**. Kevin scored 16 points in the first quarter.

The big forward put up six more points in the second quarter. Then Kevin scored three points in the third quarter. But the Denver Nuggets didn't give up. Minnesota had a small

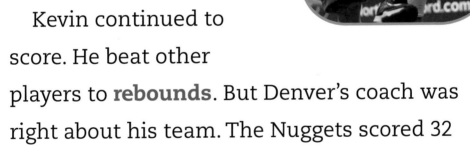

Kevin jumps for a layup.

lead, 73–69. Denver coach George Karl knew his team still had time to win. "Kevin Love's an **All-Star** player, but it's a 48 minute game," said Coach Karl.

Kevin continued to score. He beat other players to **rebounds**. But Denver's coach was right about his team. The Nuggets scored 32 points in the fourth quarter. They won the game, 101–94. Kevin scored a total of 34 points. He also grabbed 14 rebounds.

Kevin's uncle is famous rock star Mike Love of the Beach Boys.

"I haven't even practiced, so I just kind of threw myself into the game hoping something good was going to happen," Kevin said. Minnesota lost the game. But they could count on good things happening with their star player back on the court.

Minnesota coach Rick Adelman talks to Kevin during the game.

The city of Lake Oswego is near Oswego Lake in Oregon.

BASKETBALL FAMILY

Kevin Wesley Love was born September 7, 1988, in Santa Monica, California. His parents are Karen and Stan Love. Kevin has an older brother named Collin and a younger sister named Emily. The family moved to Lake Oswego, Oregon, soon after Kevin was born.

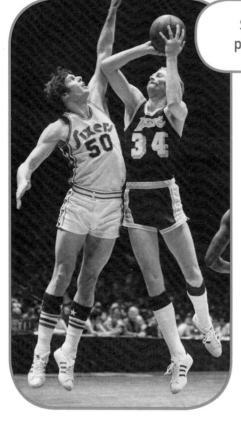

Stan Love *(right)* played in the NBA.

Stan played four seasons in the NBA in the 1970s. He taught Kevin the game. "My dad put the ball in my hands and had me working at an early age," Kevin said. His father also showed him videos of NBA greats. "My dad likes to say, when other kids were watching Big Bird, I was watching Larry Bird." Larry Bird played 13 seasons for the Boston Celtics. He is a member of the basketball **Hall of Fame**.

Stan played for the Los Angeles Lakers during the 1973–1974 season. His teammate was basketball legend Jerry West. Stan brought a Jerry West jersey home for his son. Years later, Kevin posted a photo of himself on the Internet wearing the jersey. The young Kevin in the photo is pretending to take a shot. "Doing my best Jerry West impression," Kevin posted with the photo. "Thanks for the jersey Dad."

Kevin's father taught him well. And the young player worked hard on his game. Kevin was named a starter on the Lake Oswego High School **varsity** basketball team for the 2003–2004 season. He was just a freshman. It's rare for a freshman to make the varsity team.

Kevin's father, Stan, played pro basketball for the Baltimore Bullets, the Los Angeles Lakers, and the San Antonio Spurs. The Bullets later became the Washington Wizards.

Kevin dunks the ball during a high school game.

Kevin proved that he belonged on the team. He averaged more than 13 points per game. The Lake Oswego Lakers finished the season with a 19–9 record.

The 2004–2005 season was even better for Kevin and the Lakers. They won 21 games and lost only eight. The team made it all the way to the state championship game, where they finally lost.

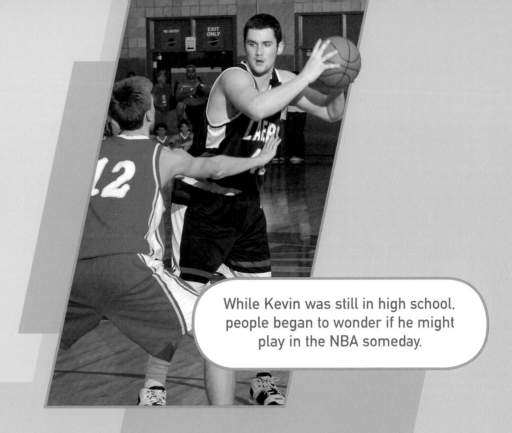

While Kevin was still in high school, people began to wonder if he might play in the NBA someday.

HIGH SCHOOL HERO

Kevin's sophomore season was a big success. He was named Oregon high school basketball Player of the Year. At a youth basketball camp, he was also voted Most Likely to Play in the NBA. But Kevin had a long way to go before he could think about joining the NBA.

The Lakers showed that they were one of the best teams in Oregon again in 2005–2006. Kevin and his teammates won 26 games. They lost only three times all year. Lake Oswego made it to the state championship game again. Kevin scored 24 points and snagged nine rebounds. Lake Oswego beat South Medford High School, 59–57. The Lakers were state champions!

Kevin celebrates his teams's victory after the 2006 state championship game.

Kevin averaged 28 points and more than 16 rebounds per game in 2005–2006. He was named Oregon Player of the Year for the second time in a row.

Kevin still had one more year of high school basketball to play. But people were beginning to wonder where he

Kevin goes up for another basket during his final year of high school basketball.

would go to college. His father had gone to the University of Oregon. Stan was one of the best scorers in Oregon Ducks basketball history. Many people thought Kevin would follow in his father's footsteps.

Kevin was a basketball star by the time he left high school.

The 2006–2007 season was another good one for Kevin and the Lakers. They won 26 games again and made it to the state championship game for the third year in a row. This time, they lost to South Medford, 58–54. Kevin was upset about the loss. But it was still a great season for the big forward. He scored more than 30 points and grabbed 17 rebounds per game. Kevin also averaged four **assists** per game.

After the season, Kevin was named Oregon Player of the Year again. This was the third year in a row he had taken home the award. He also won the Gatorade National Male Athlete of the Year award.

Kevin poses with Maya Moore at the 2007 ESPY Awards.

The University of California, Los Angeles (UCLA) has a long basketball history.

BIG MAN ON CAMPUS

There was no question that Kevin had a chance to be a star at the next level. Some **scouts** thought Kevin was the best high school player in the United States. Every college in the country would have been happy to add him to their teams. Kevin announced that he was going to UCLA.

Kevin had a good relationship with UCLA Bruins coach Ben Howland. The coach had been in touch with Kevin since the young player was in eighth grade. Kevin remembers telling Howland about his decision to join the Bruins. "When I told [Coach Howland] he almost started crying he was so happy," said Kevin.

Kevin talks to Coach Howland during practice.

There were other good reasons to choose UCLA. Famous basketball players such as Bill Walton and Lew Alcindor had played for the school. (Alcindor later changed his name to Kareem Abdul-Jabbar.) The Bruins had won the national championship 11 times. "They have a big-time tradition there," Kevin said.

Famous players such as Lew Alcindor (left) played for UCLA.

Kevin set out to add to UCLA's long basketball history. The freshman forward led his team to seven victories in a row before losing to the University of Texas. Then the Bruins won nine more games before falling to the University of Southern California (USC).

On January 24, 2008, Kevin and the Bruins traveled to Eugene, Oregon, to take on the Ducks. Kevin's father went to the game along with other family members. Stan still had good memories of playing for Oregon when he

was in college. But many Oregon fans were angry that Kevin had chosen to go to UCLA rather than play close to home.

Kevin celebrates with a teammate during a game against USC.

Kevin makes a basket against the Ducks.

People yelled cruel things at the Love family. Some held up signs with angry messages. Others threw popcorn and empty cups.

Stan was upset. "I'll never go back there," he said. Kevin put the angry fans out of his mind. He scored 26 points with 18 rebounds. The Bruins won, 80–75.

Kevin takes a shot against the University of Memphis.

GETTING BETTER

UCLA would lose only one more game during the 2007–2008 regular season. They entered the National Collegiate Athletic Association (NCAA) **tournament** in March. Kevin and the Bruins won game after game. They made it all the way to the **Final Four**. But they finally lost to the University of Memphis, 78–63.

It had been a great season for Kevin and the Bruins. But he would not be back for his sophomore year. Kevin announced in April that he was going to enter the NBA **draft**. "I feel like I'm in the right spot to take my game to the next level," he said. "Since I was five years old this has been a dream of mine."

On June 26, 2008, the Memphis Grizzlies chose Kevin with the fifth pick in the draft. They quickly traded him to Minnesota.

Kevin smiles after being chosen in the 2008 NBA draft.

The Los Angeles Lakers used to play in Minnesota. The Minneapolis Lakers moved to Los Angeles before the 1960–1961 season.

The Timberwolves were not a good team. They lost 58 games during the 2008–2009 season. They won only 24. But Kevin gave the team some hope for the future. He averaged more than 11 points per game during his rookie season. He also grabbed more than nine rebounds per game. Kevin was getting better and better. But the 2009–2010 season was even worse for the team. The Timberwolves finished with a record of 15–67.

The Timberwolves were not a good team in 2009-2010, but Kevin played hard every day.

Kevin looks to pass during a game against the Denver Nuggets.

Minnesota didn't do much better in 2010–2011. They ended the season with 17 wins and 65 losses. But Kevin was great. He took his scoring and rebounding to new levels. On November 12, 2010, Kevin scored 31 points against the New York Knicks. He also snagged 31 rebounds. No NBA player had scored

30 points and grabbed 30 rebounds in a game since Moses Malone in 1982.

"It seemed like no matter what anybody did I was going to go and get those rebounds," Kevin said after the game. "I impressed myself."

Kevin broke his hand early in the 2012–2013 season. Then he hurt his knee and had surgery. He missed most of the season.

Some of Kevin's fans cheer him on during a game.

The Timberwolves have a lot to look forward to with Kevin leading the way. "I know this team is hungry," Kevin said. "I'm hungry myself. The only thing we can do now is just look toward the future."

Kevin *(right)* and his teammates hope to make Minnesota a winning team.

Selected Career Highlights

2012–2013   Missed first weeks of season with a
           broken hand

2011–2012   Named to NBA All-Star Game for the
           second time
           Named to the All-NBA Team

2010–2011   Named to the NBA All-Star Game for
           the first time
           Named NBA Most Improved Player

2009–2010   Averaged 14 points and 11 rebounds
           per game in his second NBA season

2008–2009   Named to the NBA All-Rookie Team
           Named Western Conference Rookie of
             the Month for March
           Drafted by the Memphis Grizzlies and traded to the
             Minnesota Timberwolves

2007–2008   Led UCLA to the Final Four

2006–2007   Named Oregon basketball Player of the Year for the third
             time
           Led Lake Oswego to a state championship game for the
             third time
           Named Gatorade National Male Athlete of the Year

2005–2006   Named Oregon basketball Player of the Year for the second
             time
           Led Lake Oswego to victory in the state championship
             game

2004–2005   Named Oregon basketball Player of the Year
           Led Lake Oswego to the state championship game

2003–2004   Led Lake Oswego to a winning record as a freshman

Glossary

All-Star: one of the best players in the NBA. All-Stars play in a midseason game

assists: passes to teammates that help teammates score baskets

draft: a yearly event in which sports teams take turns choosing new players

Final Four: the name given to the last four teams at the NCAA basketball tournament each year. The Final Four team that wins two more games becomes the national champion.

forward: a player on a basketball team who usually plays close to the basket

Hall of Fame: a memorial that honors the best players in basketball history

layups: shots taken with one hand close to the basket

rebounds: grabbing missed shots

rookie: a first-year player

scouts: basketball experts who watch players closely to judge their ability

three-point shots: shots taken from behind the three-point line painted on a basketball court

tournament: a set of games held to decide the best team

varsity: the top sports team at a school

Further Reading & Websites

Birle, Pete. *Minnesota Timberwolves*. Minneapolis: MVP Books, 2013.

Kennedy, Mike, and Mark Stewart. *Swish: The Quest for Basketball's Perfect Shot*. Minneapolis: Millbrook Press, 2009.

NBA Website
http://www.nba.com/
The NBA's website provides fans with news, statistics, biographies of players and coaches, and information about games.

Official Site of the Minnesota Timberwolves
http://www.nba.com/timberwolves/
The official website of the Timberwolves includes schedules, news, and profiles of past and current players and coaches.

Official Website of Kevin Love
http://kl42.com/
Learn more about Kevin's life and career from his official website.

Sports Illustrated Kids
http://www.sikids.com/
The *Sports Illustrated Kids* website covers all sports, including basketball.

Index

Abdul-Jabbar, Kareem, 20

Bird, Larry, 10

Denver Nuggets, 5–7, 26–27

Final Four, 23

Hall of Fame, 10
Howland, Ben, 19

Los Angeles Lakers, 10–11, 25
Love, Karen (mother), 9
Love, Kevin; and injury, 5; career
    highlights, 29; childhood, 9–11;
    college career, 18–23; family
    of, 9; high school career, 11–17;
    NBA career, 4–8, 24–28
Love, Stan (father), 6, 9–11, 15,
    21–22; NBA career, 10–11

Memphis Grizzlies, 24
Minnesota Timberwolves, 4–8,
    24–28

NBA draft, 24

University of California, Los
    Angeles (UCLA), 18–22
University of Oregon, 15, 21–22

Walton, Bill, 20
West, Jerry, 11

Photo Acknowledgments

The images in this book are used with the permission of: AP Photo/Jim
Mone, pp. 4, 6, 26, 29; © Greg Smith/USA TODAY Sports, p. 5; © Kyndell
Harkness/Minneapolis Star Tribune/CORBIS, p. 7; AP Photo/Hannah Foslien,
p. 8; Esprqii/Wikimedia Commons, p.9; AP Photo/Rusty Kennedy, p. 10; Seth
Poppel Yearbook Library, p. 12; Louis Lopez/Cal Sport Media/Newscom,
pp. 13, 15, 16; AP Photo/Thomas Boyd, p. 14; © Frederick M. Brown/
Getty Images, p. 17; © Foxestacado/Dreamstime.com, p. 18; AP Photo/
Mark J. Terrill, p. 19; AP Photo, p. 20; © Stephen Dunn/Getty Images, p. 21;
© Jonathan Ferrey/Getty Images, p. 22; © Bob Donnan/USA TODAY Sports,
p. 23; AP Photo/Seth Wenig, p. 24; © Brace Hemmelgarn/USA TODAY Sports,
p. 25; © Jesse Johnson/USA TODAY Sports, p. 27; AP Photo/Genevieve Ross,
p. 28.

Front Cover: © Mark Halmas/Icon SMI.

Main body text set in Caecilia LT Std 55 Roman 16/28.
Typeface provided by Adobe Systems.